I am Muhammad Ali

I am
Muhammad Ali

By Felicia S. Hudson

Illustrated by Sophia Ian

I am Muhammad Ali

A collection of biographies from the *Who Am I Series* an OPEN UNIVERSAL LIBRARY biography

PUBLISHED 2017
by Open Universal Library.
First Edition.

ISBN: 978-1544149127

Also by Open Universal Library:

- I am Barack Obama
- I am Donald Trump
- I am Albert Einstien
- I am Justin Bieber
- I am Walt Disney
- I am LeBron James
- I am Leonardo Da Vinci

All rights reserved; no part of this book may be reproduced by any means, electronic, mechanical, photocopying or otherwise, without the prior permission of the publisher.

Copyrights © 2017
Cover and design layout by Sophia Ian
Writen and reproduced by Felicia S. Hudson Copyrights © Open Universal Library
Illustrations by Sophia Ian Copyrights © Open Universal Library

www.openuniversallibrary.com

Contents

Prologue 6

Chapter 1 — From Cassius Clay to Muhammad Ali 9

Chapter 2 — Float like a butterfly! Sting like a bee! .. 19

Chapter 3 — Refusal to the military 28

Chapter 4 — Fight of the Century 37

Chapter 5 — Rumble in the Jungle 47

Chapter 6 — Thrilla in Manila 59

Chapter 7 — The Rebuttal 70

Chapter 8 — Ali the Philanthropist 78

Chapter 9 — Parkinson's 88

Chapter 10 — Recognised and Remembered 97

Timeline 104

Bibliography 106

Prologue

The loss of a global colossus thrusts the world into mourning, remembering him not only for his outstanding professionalism, but also in the arenas of politics, religion and popular culture. On Friday night, June 3, 2016, at a hospital in Phoenix, Arizona, Muhammad Ali passed away.

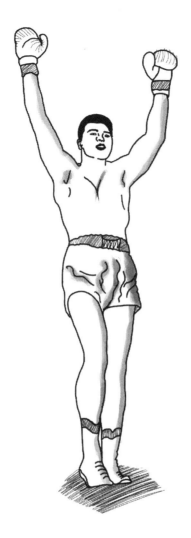

His funeral took place in his hometown of Louisville, Kentucky, where flags were lowered to half-mast on the Saturday following his death.

Ali's greatest opponents in the ring, Joe Frazier and George Foreman, were some of the mourners who grieved his death.

Luckily, Ali lived to see the first African American elected to the White House. Barack Obama paid his condolences by saying: "Like everyone else on the planet, Michelle and I mourn his passing. But we're also grateful to God for how fortunate we are to have known him, if just for a while; for how fortunate we all are that the Greatest chose to grace our time. Muhammad Ali shook up the world. And the world is better for it. We are all better for it."

Chapter 1
From Cassius Clay to Muhammad Ali

Cassius Clay was born on January 17, 1942, in Louisville, Kentucky. Young Cassius Clay was

gifted a bike by his father Cassius Clay Sr. on his twelfth birthday. However, it was promptly stolen. Ever since that day he had vowed to thrash whoever had stolen it. It was after this incident that Clay was warned by a policeman, Joe Martin, that he'd better learn to fight before he challenged anyone. After six months of training with Joe Martin, young Clay was able to win his first match in a three round decision. This event marked the beginning of the success story of the world's greatest boxer. He dedicated the rest of his life to serving his passion.

Clay had four brothers and a sister. His father, Cassius Marcellus Clay Sr. was named after the 19th century Republican politician from the state of Kentucky. He earned a living by painting billboards and signs while his mother, Odessa O'Grady Clay, worked as a domestic helper. According to her, Cassius Clay never sat still and achieved most of his milestones before his time. Children of his age walked or ran flat-footed, whereas Clay tiptoed around.

Clay finished high school at Louisville High, where he wasn't known for his academic progress, but he was certainly very popular in school because of his obsession with the sport of boxing even at his young age. He'd shadowbox in school corridors and in front of the restroom mirror. In spite of his reputation as a gifted young boxer appearing regularly in local boxing shows,

Clay was a sweet, charming and a very likable fellow. His school principal, Mr. Atwood Wilson, was particularly fond of him and when there was any sort of trouble among the students, he'd warn the students by saying something like, "Stop the crap or I'll put Cassius Clay on you!" And when Clay's teachers refused to allow him to graduate, Wilson interfered and gave an impassioned speech saying that "One day, this kid, in a single fight, will earn more than all of you earn in a year combined, and our claim to fame will be that we taught Cassius Clay." This

discourse became known in school lore as the 'Claim to Fame' speech.

Clay grew up amid racial segregation. During his teenage years, it is reported that he encountered events where he was deprived of certain facilities because of his colour. He was affected by incidents that were as a consequence of racial discrimination.

Clay was now on the verge of inclining towards anything that offered solutions, even remotely related to human rights equality, and that's when the 'Nation of Islam' came to the rescue.

He first heard about the Nation of Islam in 1959 while fighting the Golden Gloves tournament in Chicago. The Nation of Islam is an African American movement founded in Michigan, United States in 1930, which aimed at improving the mental, social and economic conditions of African Americans in the United States. Clay attended his first Nation of Islam meeting in 1961 and continued to do so while keeping his activity hidden from the public. It wasn't until 1964 that the Nation of Islam agreed to publicize Clay's membership with it and shortly after, Elijah Muhammad, leader of the Nation of Islam, announced the renaming of Cassius Clay to Muhammad Ali, which means "worthy of praise". Muhammad Ali had now officially embraced Islam and moved to Chicago, where he lived close to the Nation of Islam's Mosque (a place where Muslims worship God) and Elijah Muhammad's residence. He continued to live there for the next twelve years of his life.

Ali was married four times and had seven daughters and two sons. His first marriage was in 1964 to a waitress called Sonji Roi, which ended

after about two years, due to Ali's objections against his wife's conformity to Islamic tenets, like modest dressing.

His second marriage, in 1967, was with Belinda Boyd who, like Ali, converted to Islam and changed her name to Khalilah Ali. They had four children: Maryum, twins Jamillah and Rasheda, and Muhammad Ali Jr., born in 1972. His second marriage ended in 1977 and then he married an actress and model, Veronica Porche. They had two daughters, Hana and Laila Ali. This marriage was over nine years later, in 1986.

In 1986, he married Yolanda (Lonnie) Williams and adopted a son Asaad Amin at the age of 5 months. He also had two illegitimate daughters, Miya and Khaliah.

One of Ali's daughters, Laila, became a boxer in 1999 despite Ali's disapproval, because Muhammad Ali was strictly against female boxing since he believed women weren't made to be hit.

Muhammad Ali went on the pilgrimage (Hajj: a mandatory duty performed by Muslims once in their lifetime) to Mecca in 1972 where he met people of different colour from all over the world and enhanced his spiritual awareness.

In 1977, he publicly declared that after he retired, he would dedicate the rest of his life preparing for the hereafter by helping people, charitable causes, uniting people and helping to

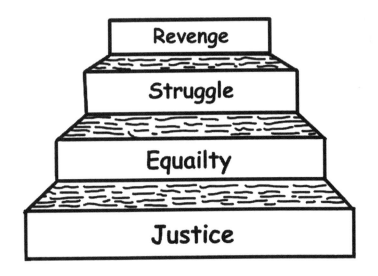

make peace. He offered another pilgrimage to Mecca in 1988.

Muhammad Ali was the man who believed that real success only comes when we rise after falling and he proved that we can make this world a better place by perennial faith and unswerving love. His death on the June 3, 2016, left his family, friends and fans in much grief.

Chapter 2
Float like a butterfly! Sting like a bee!

Clay started his boxing career at an incredibly young age and in no time he was able to accomplish a lot more than any of the other boxers of his age

could. He started his career by winning a match in a three-round decision in 1954.

The path to his greatness began shortly after his graduation in 1960, when he was invited to participate in the Rome Olympics, a life changing event. He nearly missed this event due to his fear of airplanes. But his desire to win the heavyweight title had motivated him to go. However, he insisted on bringing a parachute with him.

He successfully sailed through the first three fights of the Olympics Championship and felt greater with every victory. His final fight against Zbigniew Pietrzykowski of Poland, was rough in the first two rounds, but the last round earned him the Olympic light-heavyweight gold medal in Rome on September 5, 1960. Clay was now officially on the road to international fame and applauds.

Clay now swaggered around the Olympic village with his medal always around his neck. He cherished his victory like no one else did, and he walked, ate and even slept with his medal. He became known as the mayor at the Olympic village. "His peers loved him, everybody wanted to see him. Everybody wanted to be near him. Everybody wanted to talk to him. And he talked all the time", Wilma Rudolph, winner of three sprinting gold medals in Rome, said in an interview. Clay often used rhyme schemes and

spoken word poetry, both when he was trash talking in boxing and in political poetry for his activism outside of boxing.

Upon his return to Louisville, he was welcomed like a hero, a super star - while he was just getting started.

On October 29, 1960 he made his professional debut in his hometown of Louisville, Kentucky, winning a six round unanimous decision against

Tunney Hunsaker, whose day job was police chief of Fayetteville, West Virginia.

In February 1964, at only 22 years of age, Clay won the heavyweight title by beating Sonny Liston, an American boxer and world heavyweight champion in 1962. Although widely regarded as unbeatable, Liston lost the title after being put down by Clay in the seventh round. He wore a blue denim jacket embroidered with the words "Bear Hunter" to the arena, and incessantly shouted, "Float like a butterfly! Sting like a bee!", while banging a walking stick against the floor. His eyes nearly popped out of his skull. "I'm going to eat you alive!", he shouted at Liston when Liston entered the weigh-in. Clay, fond of using spoken words poetry and derision, labelled Liston as 'the big ugly bear' at the pre-fight weigh-in and claimed he would donate him to the zoo after defeating him. He also sent him a satirical rhyme the evening before the first fight, adding to the pre-fight publicity.

POEM

"Clay comes out to meet Liston and Liston starts to retreat,
If Liston goes back an inch farther he'll end up in a ringside seat.
Clay swings with a left,
Clay swings with a right,
Just look at young Cassius carry the fight.
Liston keeps backing but there's not enough room,
It's a matter of time until Clay lowers the boom.
Then Clay lands with a right, what a beautiful swing,
And the punch raised the bear clear out of the ring.

POEM

Liston still rising and the ref wears a frown,
But he can't start counting until Sonny comes down.
Now Liston disappears from view, the crowd is getting frantic
But our radar stations have picked him up somewhere over the Atlantic.
Who on Earth thought, when they came to the fight,
That they would witness the launching of a human satellite.
Hence the crowd did not dream, when they laid down their money,
That they would see a total eclipse of Sonny."

The second time he fought Sonny Liston was in 1965, soon after changing his name from Cassius Clay to Muhammad Ali. This fight took place in Lewiston, Maine and remains the only heavyweight title fight held in the state of Maine. With Ali being awarded the first-round knockout victory, this fight ranked as one of the shortest heavyweight title bouts in history. And the deciding blow, dubbed 'The Phantom Punch', produced one of the most famous sports photographs of all time.

Chapter 3
Refusal to the military

The United States was at war with Vietnam, ever since President John F. Kennedy decided to send military advisers to South Vietnam in 1961,

marking the beginning of the twelve year long military combat. The objective was to preserve an independent, non-communist state in South Vietnam but, it couldn't be achieved due to various diplomatic and military failures.

However, Muhammad Ali had long been an opponent of the Vietnam War, because he did not believe in going all the way to another country just to attack the brown people in Vietnam, when the so-called Negro people in his hometown, Louisville, were extremely mistreated and deprived of basic human rights.

In 1964, Ali failed the US Military qualifying test because of his poor writing and spelling skills. But after the upsurge of the Vietnam War, the test standards were lowered; qualifying Ali to be inducted into the U.S. Army in 1966. When Ali heard the news, he refused to serve the U.S. Army and openly declared himself a conscientious objector; a person who, for reasons

of conscience, objects to serve in the armed forces. Along with Ali's opposition to American involvement in the Vietnam War, he also cited his religious beliefs, saying: that "war is against the teachings of the Holy Qur'an. I'm not trying to dodge the draft. We are not supposed to take part in any wars unless declared by Allah or The Messenger. We don't take part in Christian wars or wars of any unbelievers."

The incidents that followed were certainly not in Ali's favour. On June 20, 1967, he was convicted of Draft Evasion; an intentional decision not to comply with the military conscription policies of one's nation. He was sentenced to five years of imprisonment, suspension of his boxing license for three years and imposed a fine of $10,000.

However, the appeals process kept him out of jail, but no one allowed him back in the ring, despite various efforts put in by Ali's promoters

to get his license back. They even tried to set up a fight across borders, but he wasn't permitted to leave the country.

While in exile, Ali made the most of his time by lecturing on college campuses and earning money through this means. In his speeches, he

shed light on the racial discriminations of society by relating everyday examples. He had a very opposing stance against the racial intolerance prevalent in his country. In his speeches, he went on to explain how everything white was

considered supreme and suggested that the people had been strategically brainwashed to make them believe this notion.

As Ali's stature as a political and social force grew, his popularity elevated. He was respected for never backing down from his beliefs, and endured the consequences of refusing induction to the armed forces. Soon he had gained support of the masses. Ali had challenged the system, and all those people who hated injustice were on his side.

In 1970, Ali's boxing license was reinstated by the New York State Boxing Commission, bringing Ali back to the ring on October 26, 1970. His first fight after exile was against Jerry Quarry in Atlanta, which he won by cutting Quarry out after the third round. Ali's fight style had changed when he returned to the ring; he had gone soft, his legs weaker than before and he had developed some fat. So he was no longer fast enough to dodge

most punches thrown at him. This led to the physical damage he suffered later in his career.

Chapter 4
Fight of the Century

Born in Beaufort, South Carolina, Joseph William "Joe" Frazier; the Summer Olympics Champion in 1964, had now claimed the title of World Heavyweight Champion like Ali. During Ali's absence, Joe Frazier, nicknamed 'Smokin Joe', the undefeated, had garnered two championship

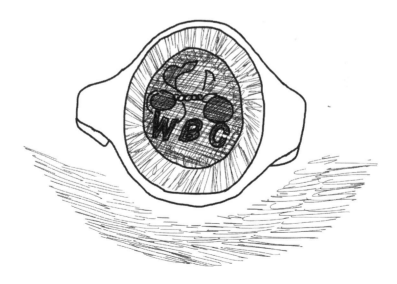

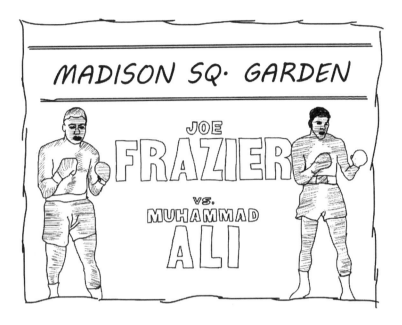

belts and was recognized by boxing authorities as World Champion.

In 1971, these two undefeated rivals, Ali and Joe, came up against one another to fight for the World Heavyweight Championship. Frazier, at that time, was well-practiced and in better shape, was famous for his left 'hook' (a boxing punch performed using core muscles) and ferocious attacking, had made him plausibly Ali's superior. While Muhammad Ali 'The Greatest', as proclaimed, charged with rigor and passion and was ready to take the challenge on the chin.

On March 8, 1971, Madison Square Garden in New York City was packed with 20,455 people, that included outrageously dressed fans, countless celebrities and media reporters, in addition to the millions watching on broadcasting screens around the world. Each seat is said to have sold for $150, bringing revenue of $1.5 million at that time, it would have been worth a lot more today. The spectators included many famous TV stars of that time and an artist, LeRoy Neiman, who painted Ali and Frazier as they fought. Anticipation was in the air; new commentators were hired by the fight's promoters, adding to the hype.

This day meant more than just a fight to the Americans. Ali, who had become an emblem of the social equality movement during his years in exile, was facing Frazier, a supporter of the

pro-war movement on a public platform infused tension amongst the masses.

The fight began with the first three rounds dominated by Ali, but towards the end of the

third round, Frazier took the lead with a whopping hook to Ali's jaw snapping his head back. Frazier began to dominate from the fourth round by

viciously attacking Ali's body and taking him to the ropes with several of his famed left hooks.

By the sixth round, Ali became tired. Frazier, taking advantage of his weakened pace, delivered tremendous body blows. However, Ali did put together a flurry of punches every now and then, while trying to dodge the blows thrown at him. Until the eleventh round, the fight seemed very competitive.

With 49 seconds to the next round, Ali was trapped in a corner and then rocked by a Frazier hook. Another hook buckled his knees as he fell into the ropes - causing uproar amongst the audience. At this moment, the referee of the fight, Arthur Mercante, dived in to separate the two.

Ali, although completely knackered, kept talking and taunting Frazier and amazingly, survived the round.

The unbeaten Frazier, 27 years old, was now up and against his mighty competitor Ali, 29 years old, ready to take the fifteenth round with full swing. Vows and screams travelling across the city, with breaths clenched, people awaited the result of the most anticipated fight, hence labelled 'the fight of the century'.

Frazier left the world thrilled by making history on the night of March 8, 1971, knocking out the great Muhammad Ali with the famous left hook. The crowd rose in agony, astonishment, having seen the former champion taken down by the current champion. The air went thicker than usual, with an uproar of emotions.

There are twosomes as well-paired as salt and pepper in every existing field, and in sports, Muhammad Ali and Joe Frazier, the famous pair, are forever linked in the memory of sports fans.

Although he lost the fight, a few months later, on June 28, 1971 he scored an important victory by overturning his draft conviction with complete support of the Supreme Court.

Chapter 5
Rumble in the Jungle

Ali's next fight against Joe Frazier was in January 1974. This fight was promoted as the 'Super Fight II', held at the same location as before - Madison Square Garden, New York City. This fight was won by Ali in the twelfth round after a unanimous decision. However, this victory was not just to take vengeance from his loss in the first

fight, but also to try his luck for the heavyweight championship against George Foreman, who had earned the title in 1973 by putting down Frazier. Thus, Super Fight II meant more to him. Ali, the greatest, was now up for a challenge against the current heavyweight champion.

After being stripped of his title and the three and a half years suspension from boxing,

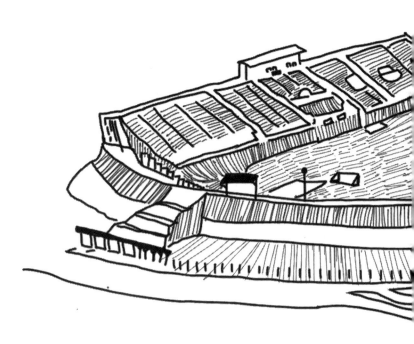

Ali decided to get back in motion shortly after regaining his boxing license. In an attempt to regain the heavyweight championship, the first comeback fights he had were fought against Jerry Quarry, Oscar Bonavena and the then undefeated heavyweight champion, Joe Frazier.

On the glorious morning of October 30, 1974, it was obvious to all 60,000 fans in the 20th of

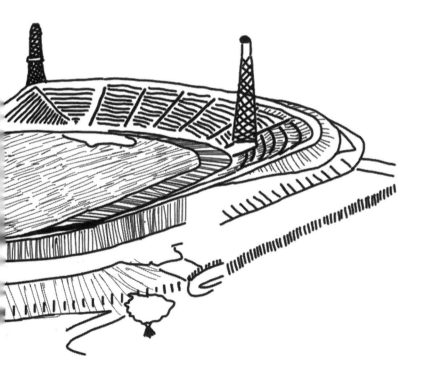

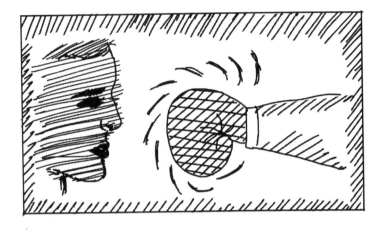

May Stadium (now the Stade Tata Raphaël) in Kinshasa, Zaire (now the Democratic Republic of Congo), and millions more watching live on closed-circuit television, that things were beginning to go horribly wrong for Muhammad Ali. What the society reckoned was the giant of a man, with a daunting specimen of gleaming muscle and cold dead eyes, George Foreman up against their very favourite, Muhammad Ali.

The fight started at 4 am in pretty much the same manner as Ali had comically predicted it would in the pre-fight press conferences, calling his robotic moves paralleled to Frankenstein's monster moves. But when he was in the ring with the champion, it didn't seem so funny after all.

Foreman pursued the former champion around the twenty foot ring, landing quirky punches and power shots that seemed too much for any man to withstand. And that's how he had been training in the months leading to the fight, thudding hundreds of successive punches into the heavy bag. Using the same tactics, he aimed inhuman blows at Ali, each one drawn to daze and destroy.

But Ali was no ordinary mortal, he was 'the greatest' for reasons well justified by his acts. Instead of wilting and losing strength, he took the fierce blows from his opponent right on the chin, and avoided the worst of Foreman's fury. Foreman is reported to have told Ali's biographer Thomas Hauser in the book *Muhammad Ali: His Life and Times* that he had hit Ali with the hardest shot he

had ever delivered to an opponent, yet he had seen Ali with the most challenging expressions. Ali had embraced each of the shots aimed at his

body with provocation and fury, with his mind and mouth working non-stop. It seemed like he was provoking George to show all he had in him, hitting the then champion's ego and emotions at every point.

Ali, despite being a controversial figure in America due to his draft dodging and association with the Nation of Islam, was dearly loved in

Africa. The reason was possibly because of his people loving nature, which he displayed by spending time at the banks of Zaire River among people. His stance against U.S. military also spoke volumes to a nation that had recently been freed of Western powers. Foreman, on the other hand, displayed a rather unfavourable nature and was

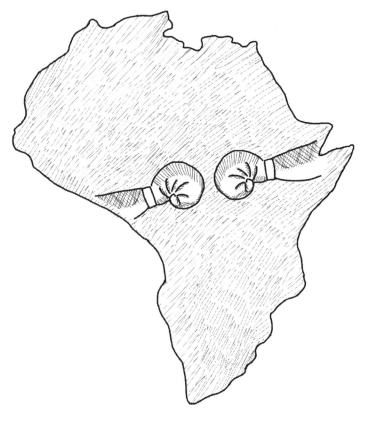

usually hard to reach. He spent most of his time with his dog, a German Shepherd.

For the fight against Foreman, Ali had planned special tactics. Although his right hand punches failed to significantly hit him, it surprised Foreman. Ali had a secret plan as the second

"I'm so fast that I can turn the light off and be in bed before the bulb goes out"

round commenced. He used a strategy called 'rope-a-dope', which allowed him to frequently lean on the ropes and cover up, meanwhile letting Foreman punch him on the arms and body. This caused Foreman to lose his strength without earning any points or even hurting Ali. The key to Ali's 'rope-a-dope' tactic was this loss of energy.

Ali then took every opportunity to shoot punches at Foreman's face, using different tactics that not only hurt Foreman, but were also earning points. All the while, taunting Foreman.

As the fight drew into the eighth round, Foreman's defence and punches had visibly

weakened. His moves became ineffective and, despite his continuous struggle to pin Ali on the ropes, he stumbled to the ropes. His tactical moves turned out to be the most brilliant of Ali's career. The referee called off the fight a few seconds before the end of the eighth round, winning Ali the heavyweight title yet another time. Three hours after a victory that bolstered his status as the most celebrated athlete, if not the most famous person, on the planet, a beaming Ali was spotted on a Zaire stoop, showing magic tricks to African children. This fight became known as the *Rumble in the Jungle*.

> *"I'm so fast that I can turn the light off and be in the bed before the bulb goes out"*
>
> – Muhammad Ali

Chapter 6
Thrilla in Manila

In March 1973, Ali lost the second of the five defeats of his career at the hands of Ken Norton

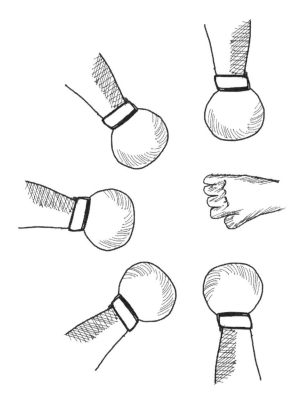

who broke Ali's jaw during the bout. Born in September, 1943, Norton held the heavyweight title from 1977 to 1978 and was best known for his classic trilogy with Muhammad Ali. Of the three, Norton was able to defeat him in the first match by a split decision, whereas Ali took the lead in the next two, which happened in September, 1973 and September 1976, respectively.

Muhammad Ali, the greatest boxer ever, lost only five fights during the span of his professional

career. Joe Frazier, Ken Norton, Leon Spinks, Larry Holmes and Trevor Berbick were the only brawny men to have defeated Ali.

In 1975 the world witnessed one of the toughest fights of Ali's career, titled as 'Thrilla in Manila'. On October 1, 1975, Ali met Joe Frazier in a fight of unrelenting aggression, considered one of the greatest fights of the twentieth century. It was held at the Metro Manila, the National Capital Region of the Philippines. The name of this contest was derived from yet another rhyming boast made by Ali during the pre-fight promotions: "it will be a killer, and a chiller, and a thriller, when I get the gorilla in Manila". Where 'gorilla' was used to refer to Ali's nickname for Frazier.

After the bout at Madison Square in 1971, when the rivals met for a rematch, neither was champion. Frazier had been put down by George Foreman, while Ali had suffered a defeat

at the hands of Ken Norton. Both were equally vulnerable. However, the pre-fight promotions sponsored by the Philippines president were executed with great zeal, because it served as

a business strategy for him. It had to divert the attention of the people from the ongoing social turmoil caused by the martial law imposition in the country. It was also during this time that Ali

had introduced his mistress, Veronica Porche, as his wife to President Ferdinand Marcos, which his wife Belinda Ali wasn't very happy about.

Since this was the third time Ali and Frazier were coming together in the ring, every bit of the anticipation was worth it. It was warm inside the Philippine Coliseum and with every passing moment, the temperature seemed to rise. With Frazier's slow starting pace, Ali took the lead in the first two rounds. He also used his 'rope-a-dope' strategy in the third round; however, it didn't work as well in Manila as it did against Foreman. However, by the fifth round, Frazier's defence improved (as Ali's worsened) and he was able to deliver solid left hooks to Ali's head, which

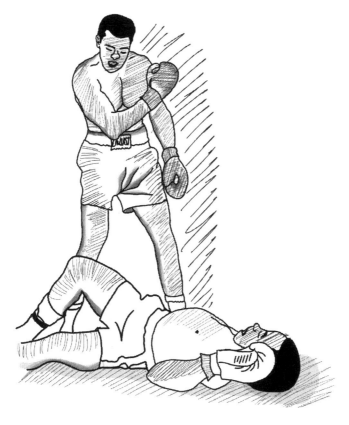

is known to be Frazier's most lethal punch. That happened shortly after the beginning of round six.

The dancing boxer, as Ali was commonly referred to, thudded Frazier with successive punches aimed at his head, causing pronounced swelling on his face by the end of the ninth round. Ali too, became visibly tired and went to his corner claiming to be the closest he had ever been to death. Towards the beginning of round thirteen, Frazier, who already had weakened eyesight ever since a training accident 1965, could now barely see.

The climax of the match came halfway through the thirteenth round when Ali smashed Frazier's gum shield right out of his mouth, hitting him

with several tremendous punches. He seemed to have used the reserves of his powers almost completely by round fourteen to ensure the match didn't pull on until the fifteenth round.

After reviewing the scores of the fourteenth round and with Frazier completely knackered, Eddie Futch, Frazier's manager for the match, signalled the referee to end the match despite Frazier's disapproval. Ali won the bout.

Later, Ali admitted that he wouldn't have been able to fight any further had Frazier not given up.

As a tribute to Ali's victory, the Philippines' first multi-level commercial mall was named "Ali Mall", standing right beside the Coliseum in which the 'Thrilla in Manila' took place.

Chapter 7
The Rebuttal

Veronica Porsche and Ali tied the knot in 1977 and with that she became his third wife.

She worked as a model and actress when she was younger and also played small parts in some popular movies of that time. She was also one of the poster girls of the promotional campaign for the 'Rumble in the Jungle'. She met Ali when she was just 18 years old, and already had their first daughter Hana, by the time they got married. Their second daughter, Laila Ali, was a rebellious child who went on to become a successful undefeated boxing champion as well as a television personality.

A documentary was also filmed about Laila, starring her own mother, Veronica. The marriage of Ali and Porsche lasted for about nine years. They divorced in 1986.

On February 15, 1978, in Las Vegas, an aging Ali lost the title to Leon Spinks in a 15 round split decision. Spinks was the winner of the light heavyweight gold medal at the 1976 Olympics Games. His match against Ali was only the eighth of his professional bouts and was ranked one of the greatest upsets in boxing history. However, just seven months later, 36 year-old Ali made

sure to strip him of the championship title in a rematch held at Louisiana on September 15, 1978. This match regained Ali his title by a unanimous fifteen round decision, making him the first ever three time heavyweight champion.

In June of 1979, Ali announced his retirement from boxing. Being a millionaire, he didn't have to worry about money, so he chose to start various ventures, like opening a fast food joint and becoming an actor. However, neither turned out to be successful. Despite the unfavourable suggestions of Ali's financial advisors who tried to leech plenty of money off him, Ali was still rich. It was during this time that president Jimmy Carter sent Ali on a diplomatic mission to Tasmania, Kenya, Nigeria, Liberia and Senegal to gain America's support in boycotting the Summer Olympics of 1980 in Moscow. However, after realising they hadn't supported Africa in boycotting the Montreal Olympics of 1976, Ali became disillusioned and returned achieving nothing. It was after the failure of this trip that he announced his comeback to the ring.

This time he came up against the heavyweight champion Larry Holmes on October 2, 1980 in Las Vegas. It was an attempt to win the heavyweight championship an unprecedented fourth time, despite some warning signs about Ali's health. In fact, it was around this time that Ali started struggling with voice stutters and trembling hands. But the Mayo Clinic declared him fit to fight and so he went. Larry was able to knock him

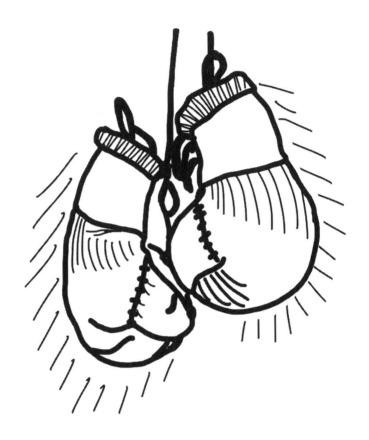

out in the eleventh round. The defeat marked the only fight Ali ever lost by knockout. This fight is said to have contributed to Ali's Parkinson's syndrome. Despite certain pleas to retire, Ali fought Trevor Berbick one last time on December 11, 1981. Ali lost by a ten round unanimous decision.

Ali, who once claimed to be able to "float like a butterfly, sting like a bee", had officially hung up the gloves in 1981, with a record of 57 wins, 5 losses and 37 knockouts. After retirement, he retreated to his Los Angeles mansion where he continued to live with his third wife Veronica.

"He who is not courageous enough to take risks will accomplish nothing in life"

– Muhammad Ali

Chapter 8
Ali the Philanthropist

Ali once said the following: "I've always wanted to be more than just a boxer. More than just the three-time heavyweight champion. I wanted to use my fame, and this face that everyone knows so well, to help uplift and inspire people around the world." Hence, the journey of his philanthropy began.

He supported causes involving numerous health disorders, medical diseases, social and domestic issues, abuse, poverty, slavery, homelessness, bullying, human rights, hunger, literacy, sports and much more. Ali worked generously with the Make-A-Wish Foundation and the Special Olympics. He visited soup kitchens and raised money through celebrity fight nights. His countless efforts for charitable causes are still remembered by millions and various programs are still effectively running because of his support and contributions. He did a lot of social work on a personal level, like delivering food and medical supplies to children in Indonesia, Morocco and

to the orphans of Liberian refugees in the Ivory Coast.

Ali travelled with Disarm Education Fund and Direct Relief International to deliver medicine and

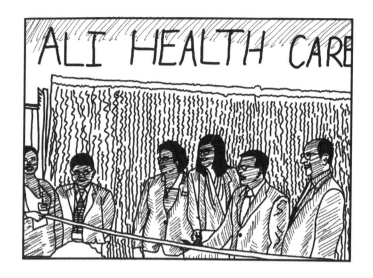

medicinal supplies worth $1.2 million to Cuba in 1998. He even went on a tour to India to raise money for various Indian charities.

Ever since his retirement in 1981, he devoted his life to helping promote world peace, civil rights, cross-cultural understanding, interfaith relations and other basic human values. He even travelled to South Africa to meet Nelson Mandela, a human rights and global peace advocate, when he was released from prison.

In 1990, he helped secure the release of 14 American hostages from Iraq during the first Gulf War. In 1998, he was chosen to be a United Nations Messenger of Peace because of his work in developing nations. President Jimmy Carter called him "Mr. International Friendship." However, his work as an ambassador of peace started back in 1985, when he flew to Lebanon

to secure the release of four hostages. He was much more than a boxer, he had political stature and was an international figure, known and praised by many.

Ali's fourth wife, Lonnie, helped him manage his business affairs, and in November 2005 she helped him open the Muhammad Ali Center in Louisville, Kentucky, an interactive museum featuring educational programming and other events to inspire children and adults to pursue

greatness in their lives and encourage people around the globe to develop integrity and respect for others. It was in the same year that President George W. Bush awarded Muhammad Ali with the Presidential Medal of Freedom.

Some of the medical causes Ali supported include HIV, Alzheimer's Disease, Cancer, Parkinson's Disease and ALS. He consequently associated himself with numerous charities and foundations that worked for this cause, like the 'Ali Care Program', 'Muhammad Ali Parkinson Center', 'Project ALS', 'UNICEF', 'Jeff Gordon Children's Foundation', 'Keep Memory Alive', and 'Make-a-Wish Foundation' to name but a few. He also annually participated in different campaigns and social events to generate funds for the Muhammad Ali Parkinson Centre, which he founded in 1997 in Phoenix, Arizona.

Today, he has passed, but his charity is alive and remembered. On that account, Muhammad

Ali received some of the world's most prestigious awards. Amnesty International, an organisation focused on human rights, awarded him with their "Lifetime Achievement Award." Kofi Annan, Secretary-General of the United Nations and former Liberty Medal recipient, bestowed him

with a citation as "United Nations Messenger of Peace."

Ali was also named "International Ambassador of Jubilee 2000," a global organization dedicated to relieving debt in developing nations. His tireless efforts bore its fruits in the form of the endorsements he received while still alive. He also lived to celebrate the longed for events of January 2009, when Barack Obama, the first black president of America, was sworn into office. It was in the same year that Ali received the President's award from the National Association for the Advancement of Coloured People – NAACP - for his public service efforts.

"Service to others is the rent you pay for your room here on earth."

– Muhammad Ali

Chapter 9
Parkinson's

However, the story of Muhammad Ali was never about boxing alone, it later became the story of a once dynamic champion battling an enfeebling disease in a way that inspired us all.

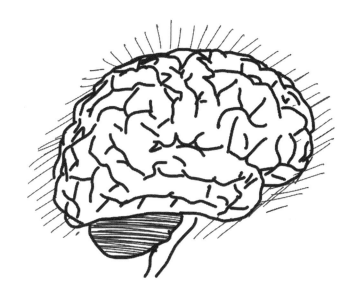

The legacy he left outside the ring remains just as important as the one inside. Three years after his retirement, in 1984, Ali was diagnosed with Parkinson's syndrome, which went on to become Parkinson's disease. In late 1970, Ali started displaying symptoms of the disease such as slurred speech and slow body movement. Even in 'Thrilla in Manila', Ali is said to have exhibited a comparatively slower pace, unlike the very quick, usual Ali.

Dr. Stanley Fahn, a neurologist specializing in Parkinson's, was the first doctor to diagnose Ali's condition in 1984. He observed a slowed blinking, decreased expression and a classic Parkinson's tremor in Ali. It is now generally accepted that the disease was caused by multiple traumas to his head, particularly in the final years of his career. Parkinson's disease is a progressive disorder of the nervous system, primarily affecting a patient's movements. It is said to affect one in five hundred people.

The disease is generally more common in older adults, but it struck Ali at the age of 42, consequently some of his symptoms were thought to be too early for typical Parkinson's and diagnosed late. The boxer, once so fleet of foot could not step ahead of his illness. But what sets him apart, was how remarkably he embraced every setback in life and rather fought it in the best possible way. Ali, being champion by all means, did what a champion should be doing.

He raised awareness about Parkinson's and became a role model for people living with the disease. Even with the progression of his illness, he remained a figure of grace under pressure. Ali, the world's most famous Parkinson's patient, helped raise $100 million for the Muhammad Ali Parkinson Centre in Phoenix.

Ali's life is an example of the life of a fighter. He suffered from permanent fatigue, he drooled and developed a tremor in his hand, yet he continued to make efforts to make the world a better place. He continued to perform his religious duties and referred to his condition as a trial from God and spoke of preparing for death. He said he used to think about it during each of his five daily prayers, but never let it show on his face. He rather seemed at peace with the idea. However, he admitted that Parkinson's had made him fearful of public speaking.

His fourth marriage to Yolanda Williams was in 1986, following the diagnosis. It was with this wife that he adopted a five month old boy, Assad Amin.

In 1996, his stage fright eased when he decided to appear on one of the biggest stages of all. He went on to light the Olympic flame at the opening ceremony of the Olympic Games in

Atlanta. The torch was handed to him by Janet Evans, the American swimmer who said, "It was all about courage. It was all around his body that he was not going to let [it] do him in. He was still the greatest." The debilitating effect of Parkinson's was evident to everyone watching the opening ceremony. His arms and upper body were seen to move vigorously as he struggled to hold the torch aloft, trying to overcome the effects of his condition, before reaching down to light the cauldron. The scene brought tears to the eyes of many present at the arena. Ali's subsequent public appearances became even more stirring as Parkinson's continued to ravage his body and mind.

His next appearance at the London Olympics 2012, as flag bearer, caused great delight amongst the fans. However, his frail appearance shocked them.

> *"I might die tomorrow, I might die next week. I don't know when I'll die."*
>
> – Muhammad Ali

Chapter 10
Recognised and Remembered

Muhammad Ali's career and overall personality were duly recognised and honoured all around the globe.

Muhammad Ali changed boxing forever. He was inducted into the boxing international Hall of Fame for his extraordinary career. He was commonly known as 'The Greatest' and won numerous awards and titles, including 'Fighter of the Year', 'Sportsman of the Year', 'Sportsman of the Century' and 'Sports Personality of the Century'.

Muhammad Ali's global presence also earned him a star on the Hollywood Walk of Fame at 6801 Hollywood Boulevard. His uniqueness is also highlighted in the famous walk, as his star reserves its place as the only star in the history of the walk that is not on the floor. As a sign of respect to his name and to preserve its sacredness, Muhammad Ali's star is on the wall next to the walk.

Ali was more than just a boxer. He also released an album in 1963 with Columbia Records called 'I Am the Greatest', which reached number 61 on the albums chart. His album was also nominated for a Grammy Award. In 1976, he released a spoken word novelty record titled 'The Adventures of Ali and His Gang vs. Mr. Tooth Decay'. This was nominated for a Grammy award in the category 'Best Recording for Children'.

The world knew that they had someone special in

Muhammad Ali. His contributions to boxing and society were recognised, appreciated and honoured well beyond his career and up to his dying moments.

Friday June 3, 2016 marked the end of an era with the death of the greatest. Muhammad Ali dedicated his life, both locally and globally, to help those in need and to work towards gender,

THE GREATEST IS GONE

economic and racial equality. Ali travelled the world to learn about its people, inspire religious tolerance and offer assistance where he could. Therefore, people from around the world mourned the end of his much applauded tenure.

Ever since the onset of Parkinson's, doctors predicted that he only had ten years left to live, but Ali's fighting spirit defied the doctors' prediction for a further 20 years as he held up against the disorder. Upon his death in 2016, people from around the world gathered in his hometown of Louisville, Kentucky to pay their condolences. He was revered and remembered globally as news

channels from every corner of the world covered his funeral and the internet was swarmed with millions of people showing their support and respect for Muhammad Ali.

Ali, who died of septic shock at the age of 74, battled on, despite becoming increasingly frail under the onslaught of the progressive disorder and beat the odds of living with the disease for more than 30 years. He was an imposing figure at 6 feet 3 inches tall and a role model too.

He will forever be remembered as truly being 'The Greatest'. Even in illness, that would

eventually lead to his death he left us with a great quote that demonstrated his humbleness and reaffirmed his place as an example to follow:

"God gave me this illness to remind me that I'm not Number One; He is,"

– Muhammad Ali

Timeline

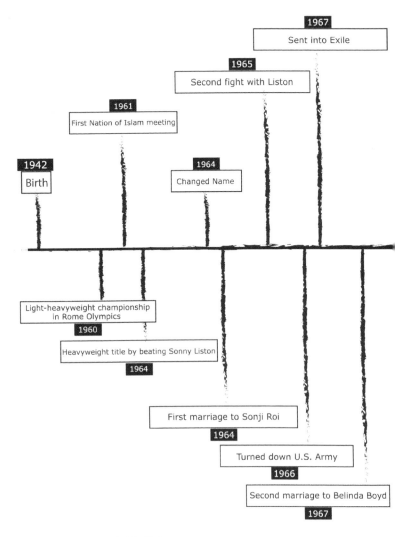

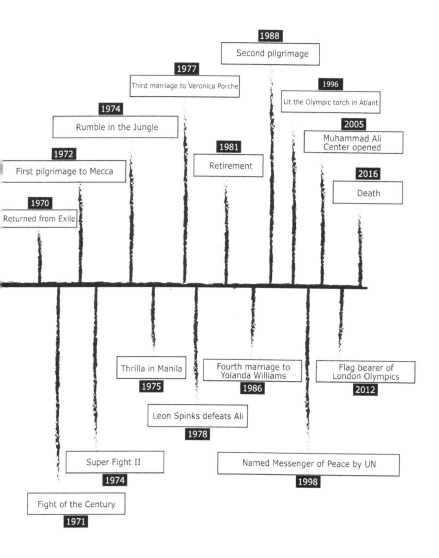

Bibliography

Hauser, Thomas. Muhammad Ali: His Life and Times. New York: Simon & Schuster, 1991.

Collins, Mark. *Muhammad Ali: Through the Eyes of the World*. New York: Skyhorse Pub., 2007.

Remnick, David. "King of the World." *Goodreads*, http://www.goodreads.com/book/show/116826.king_of_the_world.

Myers, Walter Dean. *The Greatest: Muhammad Ali*. New York, Scholastic Press, 2001.

Rolph Sugar, Bert. "Sugar: 'Fight of the Century' Was Boxing at Its Best." *USA Today*. Gannett, 04 June 2016. Web. 31 Oct. 2016.

Stevenson, Chris, and Olivia Blair. "Why Muhammad Ali Matters to Everyone." *Time*. Time, 4 June 2016. Web. 31 Oct. 2016.

Made in the USA
Columbia, SC
19 August 2017